9/97

SECRETS OF SPACE

BLACK HOLES AND SUPERNOVAE

David E. Newton

Series Editor:
Arthur Upgren, Professor of Astronomy
Wesleyan University

Twenty-First Century Books

A Division of Henry Holt and Company
New York

Twenty-First Century Books
A division of Henry Holt and Company, Inc.
115 West 18th Street
New York, New York 10011

Henry Holt® and colophon are registered trademarks of Henry Holt and Company, Inc.
Publishers since 1866

Published in Canada by Fitzhenry & Whiteside Ltd.
195 Allstate Parkway, Markham, Ontario L3R 4T8

Printed in the United States of America on acid free paper ∞.

Created and produced in association with Blackbirch Graphics, Inc.

Dedication

For Alma — a wonderful aunt and a wonderful friend.

Photo Credits

Cover (background) and page 4: ©NASA; cover (inset): ©Erich Schrempp/Photo
Researchers, Inc.; pages 6, 26, 44: ©John Foster/Science Source/Photo Researchers, Inc.;
page 11: Brown Brothers, Sterling, PA; page 13: North Wind Picture Archives; pages 15,
54: AP/Wide World Photos, Inc.; page 16: ©Bill Bachman/Photo Researchers, Inc.; pages
23, 46: ©Julian Baum/Science Photo Library/Photo Researchers, Inc.; page 24: ©David
Hardy/Science Photo Library/Photo Researchers, Inc.; page 31: ©Tony Craddock/Science
Photo Library/Photo Researchers, Inc.; pages 35, 56: Photofest; page 36: ©David
Wagner/Phototake/PNI; pages 40, 41: Photri, Inc.; page 43: ©Dennis Di Cicco/Peter
Arnold, Inc.; page 52: ©Helga Lade/Peter Arnold, Inc.

Library of Congress Cataloging-in-Publication Data

Newton, David E.
    Black holes and supernovae / David E. Newton.
       p.   cm. — (Secrets of Space)
    Includes bibliographical references and index.
    ISBN 0-8050-4477-9 (alk. paper)
    1. Black holes (Astronomy). 2. Supernovae. I. Title. II. Series.
QB843.B55N49   1997
523.8'875—dc21

96-48188
CIP

TABLE OF CONTENTS

INTRODUCTION

Humans have always been fascinated by space, but it has been only since the 1950s that technology has allowed us to actually travel beyond our Earth's atmosphere to explore the universe. What riches of knowledge this space exploration has brought us! All of the planets except Pluto have been mapped extensively, if not completely. Among the planets, only Pluto has not been visited by a space probe, and that will likely change soon. Men have walked on the Moon, and many of the satellites of Jupiter, Saturn, Uranus, and even Neptune have been investigated in detail.

We have learned the precise composition of the Sun and the atmospheres of the planets. We know more about comets, meteors, and asteroids than ever before. And many scientists now think there may be other forms of life in our galaxy and beyond.

In the *Secrets of Space* series, we journey through the wondrous world of space: our solar system, our galaxy, and our universe. It is a world seemingly without end, a world of endless fascination.

—Arthur Upgren
Professor of Astronomy
Wesleyan University

Black holes are fascinating objects that have captured the imaginations of scientists, writers, and artists for centuries. Here, an artist's conception of one kind of black hole is illustrated.

CHAPTER 1

UNRAVELING THE MYSTERY OF BLACK HOLES

The universe is filled with strange and wonderful things. There are stars that spin around on their axes 50 times per minute or faster. There are thin strings of matter less than an inch wide but more than a trillion trillion miles long. And there are spectacular veils of gas and dust that look like works of art in the heavens.

No object in the universe, however, is quite so amazing as a black hole. Scientists, science-fiction writers, and just plain ordinary people have long been captivated by these mysterious objects. Black holes have inspired bold new theories about the structure of the universe and have sparked exciting fantasies about new methods of time and space travel.

In order to imagine what a black hole is, you first have to understand some basic ideas about gravity, mass, weight, and volume.

Gravity is the force of attraction that exists between two objects. Mass is the amount of "stuff," or matter, in a body. Weight is a measure of the amount of gravity that is pulling on a mass. And volume is the amount of space that something occupies.

For example, if you have a bag of feathers and a bag of sand that are the same size, the volume of each is equal. However, the bag of sand has more mass because even in that same amount of space, the particles that make up the sand are much more tightly packed together than the particles that make up the feathers. The bag of sand also weighs more than the bag of feathers because the Earth's gravitational field pulls harder on the mass of sand than on the mass of feathers. (The larger the mass, the stronger the gravitational pull.)

To visualize a black hole, you have to think first of an object that has a mass at least three times that of our Sun—that's about three thousand trillion trillion tons. Then, you have to imagine that mass compressed until it occupies a space smaller than the point of a pin! In fact, you have to think of the mass in a space that has no volume at all! What a puzzle: An object that has almost more mass than anyone can imagine squashed down into nothing at all.

Overcoming the Pull of Gravity

The idea of a black hole is not new at all. In fact, the existence of black holes was first proposed almost two centuries ago by an English scientist named John Michell. Among other things, Michell theorized about the properties of black holes and how gravity is involved. Suppose, Michell reasoned, that we think about a cannonball fired directly upward into the air. The cannonball travels straight up for some distance and then falls back to Earth. The reason the cannonball falls back is that the Earth's mass pulls on it. Scientists call this "pulling" effect of mass gravitational attraction, or gravity. This is also what keeps the Moon orbiting around the Earth.

Next, Michell said, imagine that the cannonball moves through the air at a faster speed. Then it will travel upward a greater distance before falling back to Earth. In fact, you can keep increasing the speed of the cannonball until it travels fast enough to escape completely from the Earth's gravitational attraction. The rate of speed an object must travel in order to escape from the Earth's gravitational attraction is called its escape velocity.

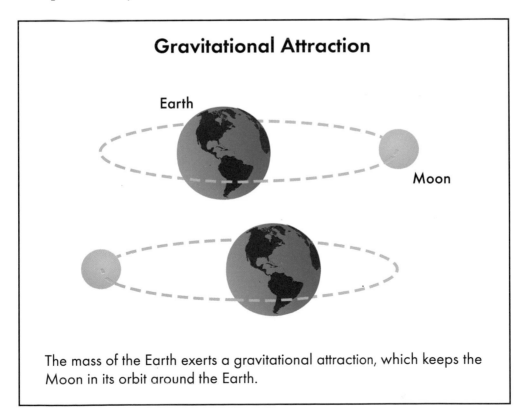

Gravitational Attraction

Earth

Moon

The mass of the Earth exerts a gravitational attraction, which keeps the Moon in its orbit around the Earth.

By Cannon to the Moon

The concept of escape velocity has been known to scientists for more than 200 years. So, it is no surprise that science-fiction writers have long used that idea in their stories. One of the most famous examples of its use is in a book written in 1865 by Jules Verne, called *From the Earth to the Moon*. In this science-fiction book, Verne describes a cannon that he claims is large enough to shoot a rocket to the Moon. He writes that the cannon is to be 900 feet (275 meters) long—the length of three football fields. It is designed to shoot a rocket 9 feet (2.7 meters) in diameter and weighing 20,000 pounds (9,000 kilograms).

Verne's story is wildly improbable. The amount of gunpowder that he calculated would be needed to fire the cannon would have blown the rocket completely apart, and would not have lifted it more than a few feet into the air.

Some of Verne's premises in this book, however, turned out to be remarkably accurate predictions of events that would occur almost a century later. He said that the cannon would be located at a site in Florida near present-day Cape Kennedy, where most U.S. space projects are carried out today. He also said that the cannon and rocket cost so much that nations around the world contributed money to build it. As it happens, international cooperation has turned out to be the key in making the world's first space station a reality; the station is scheduled for launch within the next decade.

Verne's story is still worth reading, despite its inaccuracies. The rocket is launched successfully, although it never reaches the Moon. It nearly collides with a passing meteor and is pushed off its course. It then goes into orbit around the Moon, apparently doomed to remain there forever.

The book was so successful when published that Verne followed it with a sequel in 1870 called *Around the Moon*. In the sequel, the doomed rocket has somehow found its way out of the Moon's orbit and returned to Earth, landing in the Atlantic Ocean.

An illustration from Jules Verne's From the Earth to the Moon *shows the rocket that the author imagined would travel to the Moon.*

The escape velocity of an object depends on more than speed, however. It also depends on the gravitational attraction of Earth. And the gravitational attraction of Earth, in turn, depends on its mass. What would happen, Michell wondered, if the same cannonball were fired directly upward from the Moon (which has much less mass than Earth), from the Sun (which has much more mass than Earth), or from some other body that is in space?

Since Michell lived in the eighteenth century, he didn't have the exact answers to his own questions. But scientists today do. The Moon has a gravitational attraction of only about one sixth that of Earth. So, the Moon would exert less pull on a cannonball shot into the air than does Earth. The escape velocity on the Moon is about 1.5 miles (2.4 kilometers) per second as compared to an escape velocity of almost 7 miles (11 kilometers) per second on Earth. On the Sun, the opposite is true. The Sun's gravitational attraction is nearly 30 times that of the Earth. The escape velocity on the Sun is more than 385 miles (619 kilometers) per second.

Gravity and Light

As he wondered, Michell theorized about the most extreme circumstances. Imagine, he said, a star that has so much mass that you could never fire a cannonball fast enough for it to be capable of escaping from the star's gravitational attraction. No matter how fast you made the cannonball go, the star's gravity would always be strong enough to pull the cannonball back down again.

Michell then carried his idea one step farther. Think not about a fast-moving cannonball, he said, but a beam of light. (A beam of light can be thought of as a stream of very rapidly moving particles called photons. A photon is a tiny "package" of light, just as a cannonball is a "package" of matter. The only difference is that the photon has no mass at all. Comparing a beam of light to a fast-moving cannonball was not completely correct, but Michell achieved noteworthy results.) Michell next imagined an astronomical body with a mass so large that even a beam of light could not escape from its gravitational field. No one outside the body

Pierre Simon Laplace believed that certain objects in the universe had such strong gravitational fields that even light could not escape from them.

would be able to see the object because no light could escape from it. So no one would know that the object was even there!

In 1796, a few years after Michell theorized about gravity and light, the French scientist Pierre Simon Laplace had an idea that was very much like Michell's.

The Man Who Named Black Holes

What's in a name? In the case of black holes: quite a lot. When John Archibald Wheeler invented the term black hole in 1967, he made an abstract subject that was previously of interest only to astronomers a topic that fascinated the general public. Science-fiction writers began to imagine all kinds of ways in which black holes could be used for space travel. In most cases, the writers were misguided, but the stories they wrote were interesting nonetheless.

John Archibald Wheeler was born in Jacksonville, Florida, on July 9, 1911. He earned his Ph.D. at Baltimore's Johns Hopkins University at the age of 22, continued his studies in Copenhagen, Denmark, for two years, and then joined the faculty at Princeton University in New Jersey. Wheeler has made contributions in a number of scientific fields. For example, he worked with physicist Niels Bohr on splitting atoms—the theory of atomic fission—and predicted the existence of a new element, plutonium, which was later discovered by chemist Glenn Seaborg and physicist Edwin McMillan.

Wheeler is probably best known, however, for his work in astronomy. In the years after World War II, he studied the

Laplace wrote:

> There exist in the heavens therefore dark bodies, as large as and perhaps as numerous as the stars themselves. Rays from a luminous star having the same density as the Earth and a diameter 250 times that of the Sun would not reach us because of its gravitational attraction; it is therefore possible that the largest luminous bodies in the Universe may be invisible for this reason.

behavior of matter as it collapses into smaller and smaller volumes. He suggested that it might be possible for a star, for example, to collapse so completely onto itself that all of its mass would be concentrated at a single point. Many of Wheeler's colleagues doubted that such an event was possible, although the discovery of black holes makes his theory easier to accept.

Besides inventing the term black hole, Wheeler has added other clever new words to the language of astronomy. For example, the term he suggests to label a connection that may exist between two different universes is called a wormhole.

John Archibald Wheeler

For nearly two centuries, no one thought very much about the theories of Michell and Laplace. It was difficult to imagine an astronomical body so massive that it could trap light inside of itself. Also there was no way to search for such an object in the heavens. If you couldn't see such a huge star, how could you ever find it? It was not until 1967 that such a body even had a name. Then, the American physicist John Archibald Wheeler suggested that such objects be called black holes.

Astronomers use equipment, such as this radio telescope, to help them chart the universe.

CHAPTER 2

LOOKING FOR THE INVISIBLE

Have you ever looked at the sky on a perfectly dark night?
You have to choose a night with no visible Moon and a location far from city lights. Under such circumstances, the sky
appears to be alive with stars. And astronomers have learned
that many of those sparkling points of light are not even
separate stars. Instead, they are galaxies, groups of millions
upon millions of individual stars, so far away that they appear
to us no larger than a single point.

The starry show on such a night is only a hint, however, of
what the universe is really like. Untold billions of objects in
the sky give off not only visible light, but other forms of invisible light called radiation. These are things such as radio waves,
infrared radiation, and X rays. These forms of radiation are not
visible to the human eye. Astronomers have developed special

kinds of telescopes that capture these forms of radiation and convert them to signals that we can read.

Radio telescopes, infrared telescopes, and X-ray telescopes, however, are not much help in looking for black holes. Remember that the gravitational force of black holes is so strong even light cannot escape from them. But neither can radio waves, infrared radiation, X rays, or any other form of radiation. How can an astronomer find an object that gives off no radiation?

Gravitational Lenses

One trick astronomers use to search for black holes is called a gravitational lens. Imagine that a star very far away from Earth sends out light rays that pass near a black hole. Those light rays will be bent by the strong gravitational pull of the black hole. The drawing on page 19 shows how this happens.

Notice the direction in which the light rays strike Earth. An observer on Earth assumes that the light rays are traveling in a straight line—to the human eye, light rays always appear to travel in straight lines. In this drawing, the dotted line shows the direction in which the light rays from the star *seem* to be coming. That is, the star appears to be in a location different from its true location.

You probably have had an experience like this without realizing it. Have you ever tried to pick up an object at the bottom of a pool or a stream of water? If so, you know that the object actually looks as if it's in a place different from where it really is. You grab for the object where your eyes tell you to grab, but the object is not quite there.

Gravitational Lens

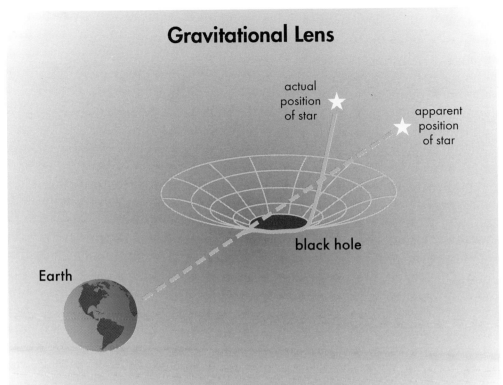

actual position of star

apparent position of star

black hole

Earth

Light rays from a star can be bent by black holes. Observers on Earth would not realize they are not viewing the actual position of the star.

Astronomers can take the gravitational lens effect into account when searching for black holes. They have charts that say where stars are located in the sky. They can point their telescopes at certain locations and expect to find certain stars there. If the stars are found to be slightly out of place, the reason may be a black hole. Light from the displaced stars may have passed a black hole and may have been bent out of a straight line.

Unfortunately, this effect is very difficult to observe. Astronomers have not yet found any "displaced" stars that might lead to the discovery of a black hole.

Peeking Through a Keyhole

The study of black holes has produced some truly remarkable predictions. One such prediction is the existence of objects known as mini-black holes.

In theory, black holes can exist in any size—from the size of the universe to the size of a proton. All that matters is that there be a very large mass for the size of the hole.

It would be possible, for example, to imagine a black hole no larger than the center of a single hydrogen atom, but with a mass equal to that of a mountain. A black hole with these properties is called a mini-black hole.

Mini-black holes have some properties that are very different from larger black holes. For example, such mini-black holes can give off radiation. Of course, the definition of a black hole says that nothing can escape from the hole, not even radiation.

But very small objects, such as a mini-black hole, are not governed by the ordinary physical laws that operate in the world around us and in the vast dimensions of outer space. Instead, they are controlled by the laws of quantum physics.

One of the laws of quantum physics says that a beam of light can change instantaneously into a pair of particles. In a mini-black hole, one of the particles created in this way falls back into the

Giant Vacuum Cleaners in the Sky

Astronomers have had more success with a second method for finding black holes. This method is based on the fact that the strong gravitational force of a black hole sucks in any and all matter that comes close to it. A black hole is, in a way, a giant vacuum cleaner that gobbles up matter around it.

hole. But the other particle is able to escape from the hole. To an outside observer, it would seem that the mini-black hole is "leaking" matter to the outside world. This conclusion may seem to conflict with everything that has been said about black holes so far. And it *is* in conflict with the usual laws of physics that deal with large-scale phenomena. According to the laws of quantum physics, however, it is permitted.

Calculations show that the rate at which mini-black holes leak increases as the hole gets smaller. At the very end of its life, a mini-black hole leaks matter so fast that it actually explodes. An exploding mini-black hole releases so much energy that it can be compared on a small scale to the Big Bang, the giant explosion in which the universe was created.

Imagine how exciting it would be, then, for an astronomer to watch a mini-black hole explode! It would create a picture of what the Big Bang was like, only on a smaller scale. It would be almost like peeking through a tiny keyhole at the most dramatic event that ever occurred in our universe—its very creation.

Some astronomers now believe that mini-black holes are especially common in certain parts of the universe, such as in the outer parts of our own Milky Way. If that's the case, it may be possible to find one, observe its final days, and, in the process, have a look at an event comparable to the Big Bang itself.

At first, this fact would not seem to be of much significant help. The universe is much more full of nothing than it is of matter. That is, if you were able to travel through space in a rocket ship, you would see no more than an atom or two every few hundred or thousand miles. Most of the time, a black hole would not find too many objects or matter to pull into itself.

One important exception exists: a binary star system. A binary star system consists of two stars that revolve around each other. Such systems are well known to astronomers; many of the stars you see in the sky on a dark night are probably binary stars. In many cases, a binary star system consists of two ordinary stars, like our Sun, spinning around each other.

What do you suppose would happen if one part of the binary star system was a black hole? In that case, we might expect the black hole to pull matter off its partner. If we could actually watch this process, it might be very exciting. Little by little, bits and pieces of the ordinary star's outer portion would get torn off by the black hole. The process would take place slowly at first because the star exerts its own massive force of attraction over its outer layers. You can imagine a kind of tug-of-war between the star and its black hole companion.

But the gravitational attraction of the black hole is much greater than that of the star, and it would pull into itself the outer layers of the star. As the black hole increased its mass and the star decreased in mass, the pieces torn off the star would fall toward the black hole at a faster rate. Eventually, they would be pulled into the black hole at the speed of light, perhaps giving off a burst of radiation just before disappearing into the hole.

And that *is* what astronomers have observed! On December 12, 1970, the National Aeronautics and Space Administration (NASA) launched a satellite named *Uhuru* into space. The satellite, whose name means "freedom" in Swahili, was built to look for X rays in the universe. (The Swahili name was chosen because the satellite was launched from the east coast of Africa.)

Black Holes Everywhere

Some astronomers today still doubt that black holes really exist. But evidence for the existence of these strange objects continues to be found. As of early 1996, astronomers had discovered at least seven objects in space that are good candidates to be black holes. The most massive of these was found in the galaxy NGC 3115. It has a mass two billion times that of our own Sun. The stars around this black hole (if that's what it is) orbit the hole at the speed of 600 miles (965 kilometers) per second.

Other astronomers now think that black holes will be found at the center of many galaxies. Researchers have found a spot in the constellation Sagittarius that they think could be a black hole at the center of our own galaxy. Stars in the region are traveling at hundreds of miles per second. Researchers calculate that the hole must have a mass of a million suns to make the stars move that rapidly.

A new approach for looking at black holes may provide even more information. We know that it is not possible to see much of anything by looking directly *at* a black hole. But it should be possible to detect black holes by observing what happens in the regions around them. For example, if one were to observe large masses of hot matter flowing rapidly into an apparently empty location in space, one might assume that the "empty" space is really a black hole. Using this technique, a Japanese X-ray satellite located a new black hole candidate at the center of the galaxy known as MGC-6-30-15 in late 1995.

This artist's conception of a black hole at the center of our galaxy shows how the hole draws matter around it into itself.

Less than a year after it reached orbit, *Uhuru* discovered an especially interesting X-ray source in the constellation of Cygnus. The X rays came from a location where no known star had been found. The location was very close to a known star, however, one with the name HDE 226 868.

HDE 226 868 is not an especially interesting or unusual star. It is about 20 times as large as our own Sun, but not very different from other stars in the universe.

By measuring the movement of HDE 226 868, astronomers were able to discover that the star had an invisible companion. It was part of a binary star system. Moreover, they were able to calculate the size and mass of the companion star. They determined that HDE 226 868's invisible companion has a mass about 10 times that of our Sun but is no larger in size than our own Earth. The companion fits the description of a black hole!

But how does this explain the X rays observed by *Uhuru?* Here is what astronomers believe is happening: HDE 226 868's black hole companion is pulling material off the larger star's

As seen in this illustration, the star HDE 226 868 (on left) is being pulled into the black hole known as Cygnus X-1 (right).

Black Holes as Energy Sources

Scientists are constantly thinking about ways to make use of black holes. (And science-fiction writers have some theories as well.) For example, some people believe black holes can be used for time travel—to go backward or forward in time.

Another suggestion has been to use mini-black holes as sources of energy. Physicist Stephen Hawking has estimated that a single mini-black hole could generate 6,000 megawatts of energy per second, an amount equal to the output of six large nuclear power plants. Suppose that we could find a mini-black hole in our own solar system. Then imagine that we could find a way to tow that mini-black hole and place it into orbit around the Earth. Perhaps we could capture the energy released by it for our own use.

This idea may seem attractive, but the obstacles are numerous. To begin with, simply finding a mini-black hole would be difficult. Then, it's not clear how the mini-black hole could actually be towed. Finally, if the mini-black hole were slightly too large, it would be likely to explode, releasing all its energy at once, rather than a little at a time. Commercial power plants probably don't have to worry about going out of business just yet!

outer shell. As that material falls toward the black hole, it spins faster and faster as it approaches the hole itself. The spinning layers of stolen matter rub against each other, giving off X rays.

Many astronomers now believe that HDE 226 868's companion, called Cygnus X-1, is the very first black hole to have been observed by astronomers. Other astronomers, however, are not convinced and think the X rays may come from another source. Eventually, enough information will become available to answer that question one way or another.

The Moon stays in orbit around the Earth because of the Earth's gravitational attraction.

CHAPTER 3

DID NEWTON'S APPLE REALLY FALL?

The concept of gravity is familiar to almost everyone today. We say that an apple falls off a tree because of gravity. And we believe that planets stay in orbit around the Sun because of gravitational forces as well.

This concept of gravity was first developed by Sir Isaac Newton in about 1666. In fact, Newton was the first person to show that the forms of gravity we know so well on Earth (such as apples falling off trees) are no different from forces acting on bodies in the sky (such as the Moon orbiting Earth).

John Michell and Pierre Simon Laplace both used Newton's theory of gravitation to discuss black holes. Scientists now know, however, that Newton's ideas about gravity are not accurate enough to describe many things that occur in the universe. Instead, they use another method of describing nature—a theory developed by Albert Einstein in the early part of this century.

A New Way to Look at Gravity

According to Einstein, space has a shape that is affected by objects. To understand this concept, imagine some region of the universe that is totally empty. No bodies of any kind are present. Einstein said that space in such a region could be pictured as a perfectly flat surface, like the top of a tight rubber sheet. If a beam of light were to travel across this region, it would follow a perfectly straight line.

Einstein also theorized that the presence of an object in space changes the shape of space around the object. Furthermore, the more massive a body is, the more it affects the shape of space. A simple way to imagine this effect is to suppose that a body is placed on top of the flat rubber sheet. The body would sink into the sheet, changing its shape. And, the more massive the body is, the more it changes the shape of the sheet.

The diagram on page 29 shows a region of space containing two bodies. Body B is more massive than body A. So the space around body B is affected more than the space around body A.

But what happens to a beam of light traveling across this region of space? As the light nears body A, its path will be deflected towards the "dent" in the surface. Its path will be deflected even more as it approaches body B because body B is more massive than body A.

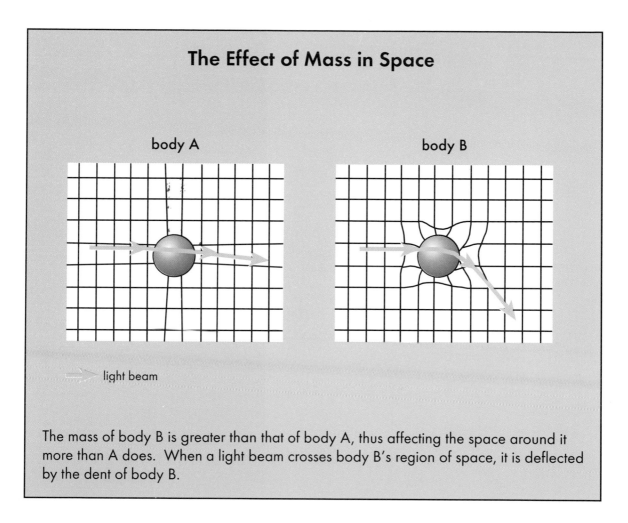

The Effect of Mass in Space

body A

body B

light beam

The mass of body B is greater than that of body A, thus affecting the space around it more than A does. When a light beam crosses body B's region of space, it is deflected by the dent of body B.

This diagram tells us what we already know about the effects of gravity. An object such as body A seems to exert a force on anything passing near it, such as a beam of light. And a more massive object, such as body B, exerts a stronger force. Both bodies change the direction of anything traveling in their vicinity.

What this type of diagram can also do, however, is make it very clear how a black hole affects any object passing near it. The drawing on page 30 illustrates this point.

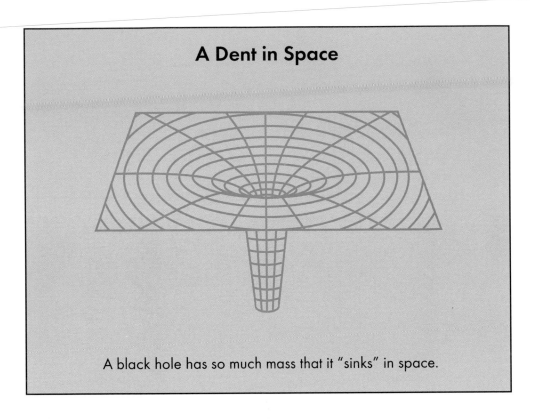

A Dent in Space

A black hole has so much mass that it "sinks" in space.

The "dent" in the diagram seen above is caused by a black hole. In this case, the black hole is so massive that objects passing close to it are not just deflected, they are swallowed up. A beam of light that gets too near the black hole will fall into it, never to return again.

Wormholes, White Holes, and Alternative Universes

The above diagram raises some very interesting questions. For instance, if a beam of light gets swallowed up by a black hole, where does it end up? One answer is that the beam keeps going and comes out "the other side" of the black hole.

The other side of a black hole, or the bottom half, is just the opposite of its top. Objects that enter the black hole at the top come streaming out at the bottom. Instead of capturing objects and light as a black hole does, the hole at the bottom gives off objects and light. Because it constantly gives off light, the hole at the bottom is called a white hole. The connection

A white hole, as illustrated here, releases energy into space.

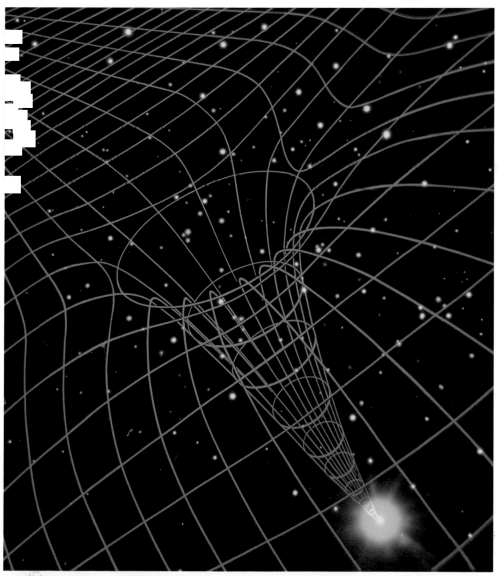

between the black hole and the white hole is called a wormhole, for reasons you can probably guess.

A white hole answers the question of where objects go when they fall into a black hole. But it raises a new question. Where do we look for the other end of the wormhole, the white hole?

The answer is rather surprising. Some astronomers think that white holes are to be found in an "alternative" or "parallel" universe. By these terms, they mean some place other than the universe we are already familiar with. It could be a universe with properties that we can only guess at, a universe somewhere backward or forward in time, perhaps. Or, it could also be a part of our own universe that we have not discovered yet.

The figure on page 33 illustrates this possibility. Suppose that our universe is curved, like an enormous donut. Then black holes might exist in the part of the universe that we can see. But white holes would be in another part of our universe that is undiscovered as yet.

Another possibility posed is that black holes may exist in a universe other than the one we know to exist. If so, they may actually be attached to white holes in the universe that we do know. Where are those white holes? The answer is that no one knows. After all, some astronomers are still debating about the existence of black holes in our universe. When scientists finally agree on that question, the search for white holes may actually begin.

At this point, some interesting candidates for white holes exist. The brightest objects in the universe, for example, are quasars. Quasars emit millions of times as much energy as our

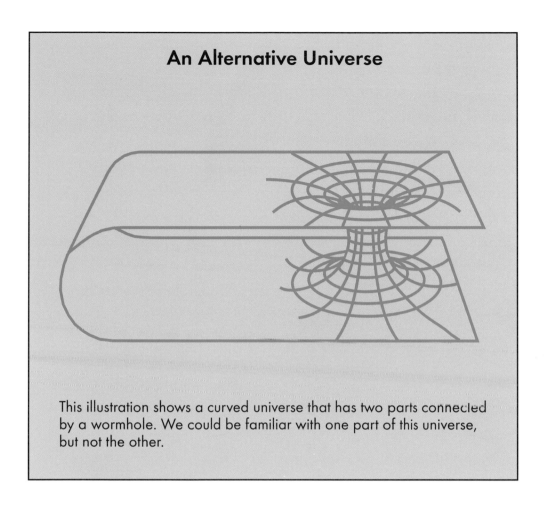

An Alternative Universe

This illustration shows a curved universe that has two parts connected by a wormhole. We could be familiar with one part of this universe, but not the other.

own Sun over areas smaller than our solar system. We do not know very much about quasars. Is it possible that one or more of them are white holes?

Perhaps you can now see why black holes are of such interest to science-fiction writers. Imagine a space traveler who falls into a black hole and travels through the wormhole. Where would that space traveler come back out: In another part of our universe? In an entirely different universe? In the present? Or in some other time completely?

"Back to the Future"

Time travel has long been a very popular topic for many science-fiction writers. In the 1985 movie *Back to the Future*, for example, actors Michael J. Fox and Christopher Lloyd play characters who use a converted automobile to travel in time. Fox's character eventually meets his mother and father before they are married.

Some writers think black holes may be the time machines we need to go forward or backward in history. This belief is supported by the diagrams in this chapter; they are really simplified versions of Einstein's time-space continuum. *Time-space continuum* refers to Einstein's theory that it takes four dimensions to represent the universe accurately. In order to talk about the motion of a planet in its orbit or a beam of light traveling across the sky, we have to describe how the planet or the light beam travel through both space and time at the same time.

What this means is that an object traveling through a wormhole changes not only the direction in which it is moving (up/down, left/right, forward/backward), but also the time in which it is traveling (forward/backward). (Remember, the idea of a "parallel" or "alternative" universe means for every "down" in our universe, there is an "up" in the parallel universe.) An object might enter a black hole today and come out tomorrow or yesterday. And that's what time machines and time travel are all about!

The only problem with this theory of time travel is what happens to an object once it is *inside* the wormhole. Remember how strong the gravitational attraction of a black hole is. It is so strong that nothing can escape from it. A light beam *might* be able to pass through a wormhole without damage. But a spaceship or a person would never be able to survive the trip—they would be torn apart by the forces of gravity inside the wormhole. Perhaps the atoms that the ship or person was made of would eventually make it out the other side. But due to the tremendous force of the wormhole, they would no longer be connected with each other in any way. What was once the spaceship or the person would become unrecognizable.

The idea of a trip into a black hole might be interesting and exciting for a while. But due to the tremendous force of the hole, it would not have a very pleasant ending for a space traveler like you or me!

Christopher Lloyd (left) and Michael J. Fox (right) play time travelers who use an automobile to go backward and forward in time in Back to the Future.

An artist's impression of an exploding supernova shows the star and the
intense energy that is released as white, green, and yellow beams of light.

CHAPTER 4

STELLAR GRAVEYARDS

"Thy ever constant skies . . ." That poetic line expresses the view that many people have of the heavens. Humans have been watching the same stars for thousands of years, and to us, nothing ever seems to change in our sky.

But like everything else in nature, stars do change. The change occurs so slowly that we are seldom aware of it. Every now and then, however, something so dramatic occurs in the skies that no one can doubt the possibility of change. One of those tremendous events is a supernova.

A supernova occurs when a star blows itself apart at the end of its lifetime. The explosion is so spectacular that it can often be seen in the middle of the day. Enough light is produced to be visible even in the presence of sunlight.

A Tug of War in the Stars

But what happens before a supernova occurs? The early lifetime of most stars is fairly predictable. When they are young, they release huge amounts of energy by means of nuclear fusion reactions. In a nuclear fusion reaction, two or more small particles combine to make a single larger particle. Probably the most common type of fusion reaction occurs when four hydrogen atoms combine to form a single atom of helium. This reaction takes place in a series of steps during which large amounts of energy are also produced. The sunlight that floods our Earth every day is produced originally by this kind of hydrogen-to-helium reaction.

Nuclear fusion reactions tend to blow stars apart. They release so much energy that portions of the star are constantly being hurtled into space. So, what prevents the star from coming apart entirely? The answer to that question is already familiar to you: gravity. The particles of which a star is made all feel a strong gravitational attraction to each other. Gravity tends to pull these particles back toward each other and toward the center of the star.

As long as the inward force of gravity and the outward force of nuclear fusion balance each other, a star can remain stable. It continues to give off light and other forms of energy as it remains in one piece.

Stellar Old Age

Most stars spend millions or billions of years in stable condition. In many cases, however, changes eventually begin to occur. The materials needed to keep the fusion reactions going (such as hydrogen atoms) are eventually used up. Gravitational forces then begin to overwhelm fusion forces, and the star begins to collapse. At this point, new fusion reactions start up. For example, helium atoms may combine with each other to form carbon or oxygen atoms. A new source of energy is found, and the star begins to expand.

Stars typically go through a number of shrinking and expanding stages like this. Each stage becomes more dramatic, however, with hotter temperatures produced within the star's core and more energy given off.

The Very End

The way a star ends its life depends on how massive it was to begin with. For example, astronomers believe that stars with masses less than that of the Sun essentially have very long lives. They just continuously generate energy from hydrogen-to-helium fusion reactions.

Stars about the size of our Sun have a different fate, however. At some point, they can no longer sustain nuclear fusion reactions. Gravitational forces are no longer strong enough for the star cores to hold on to their outer envelopes of dust and gases. This dust and gas—now known as a planetary nebula—floats off into the sky like the smoke ring from an enormous cigar. The compact center of the star, with the "ashes" of earlier fusion reactions, is all that is left behind. This central core is known as a white dwarf. The sequence of events described here is what our own Sun can expect in its future. Someday, billions of years in the future, it too will end up as a white dwarf.

The Supernova of 1987

February 24, 1987, was a historic date in modern astronomy. On that date, the first supernova visible to the naked eye since 1604 was discovered at the edge of the Large Magellanic Cloud galaxy. The supernova was first observed by Canadian astronomer Ian Shelton.

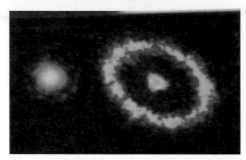

A ring of material was left around the remains of SN1987A, seen here at right. (The star at left is not part of the supernova.)

Shelton, who was working at an observatory in Chile, notified colleagues around the world, and all available telescopes were soon trained on the event.

SN1987A, as the supernova was named, both delighted and puzzled astronomers. They had been waiting for almost 300 years to see such a dramatic stellar event. Yet, when it finally occurred, it was different than had been expected. For example, the supernova appeared to have come from a type of star known as a blue supergiant. Yet, astronomers had come to believe that supernovae are formed only when red supergiants explode.

One of the most exciting discoveries associated with SN1987A was the flood of neutrinos it sent to Earth. Neutrinos are very tiny particles that scientists have sought for decades. The term *neutrino* means "little neutron" in Italian. It comes from the fact that, like neutrons, they have no electrical charge. However, they are much, much smaller than neutrons. Since they have little or no mass, they are said to be "little" neutrons.

Scientists believe that every square inch of the Earth is bombarded constantly with billions of neutrinos. However, since they have no electrical charge and virtually no mass, they are very difficult to detect.

Yet, in the days following the explosion of SN1987A, detectors in Japan and Ohio registered 19 separate neutrinos. That number, although small, constitutes a "flood" in view of how difficult the particles are to observe. For astronomers, this discovery was very important since it was the first time neutrinos had ever been detected in an exploding star.

Stars larger than the Sun experience the most dramatic endings of all. During the last seconds of their lifetimes, their cores collapse completely. Their internal temperatures rise to 35 billion°F (5 billion°C) almost instantaneously. The atoms of which their cores are composed are torn apart.

The fragments of those exploded atoms are protons, electrons, and neutrons. Protons are tiny particles that each carry a single unit of positive electricity. Electrons are particles that carry a single unit of negative electricity. And neutrons are tiny uncharged particles. Under extreme conditions like those

Colorful dust and gases make up the Great Orion nebula.

Dire Warnings from the Heavens

"Drought, increases of prices, and famine occurred. At the time when the spectacle appeared calamity and destruction occurred which lasted for many years."

It was with these words that the Muslim scholar Ali Ibn Ridwan described the supernova of the year 1006. Since the time the supernova had appeared near the constellation Scorpius—considered an unlucky sign in the Muslim religion—wars had broken out across the land.

It is no wonder that people have reacted so strongly to supernovae. Any star that shines brightly enough to be seen during the day is hard to ignore. In cultures where the heavens are thought to have profound influence on human life, such an event can easily be taken as a dramatic sign from the gods.

The very first recorded supernova in human history occurred in the year 185. A Chinese observer described the star and then told of its consequences.

"When we came to the sixth year [following the supernova]," he wrote, "the governor of the metropolitan region, Yuan-Shou, punished and eliminated the middle officials. Wu-kuang attacked and killed Ho-miao, the general of chariots and cavalry, and several thousand people were killed." There was no doubt in the observer's mind that these terrible events could all be traced to the appearance of the supernova six years earlier.

In 1054, perhaps the most famous supernova of all was reported by astronomers in China, Japan, and Arabia. But it was not mentioned by European observers. That supernova is especially famous because its remnants can still be seen today. The wispy mass of gas and dust that we call the Crab Nebula (located in the constellation Taurus) is, in fact, the remnants of the 1054 supernova.

When it occurred in 1054, the explosion raised great fears among observers.

A physician living in Baghdad, for example, wrote:

> One of the well-known epidemics of our time is that which occurred when the spectacular star appeared . . . in the year 1054. In the autumn of that year fourteen thousand people were buried. . . . Then, in mid-summer of the [following year], the Nile was low and most people . . . and all strangers died, except those whom Allah willed to live.

In most cultures today, people have given up the belief that dramatic events in the heavens determine the fate of human beings living here on Earth. Instead of fearing these spectacular events, supernovae today are appreciated for having a special beauty and wonder all their own.

In 1987, astronomers were able to observe a supernova in the Large Magellanic Cloud galaxy. The brightest star seen here (upper left) is the remnants of the supernova.

described here, protons and electrons are welded together to form neutrons. At the same time, neutrinos are released in massive amounts and travel across the universe.

The energy released during these last moments of a star's life produces one of the most dramatic explosions a universe will experience. Everything outside the very center of the star itself is blown into space, as with an enormous explosion of dynamite. So much energy is released that the exploding star can be seen during the middle of a sunlit day. If a supernova were visible above where you are on Earth today, it would appear to be shining at noon in the sky like a bright star . . . which is exactly what it is.

An exploding supernova, as seen in this artist's illustration, releases a tremendous amount of energy and affects stellar objects near it.

Once a supernova has been produced, all that is left behind, now cold and lifeless, is the star's burned-out core. It consists of nothing other than countless numbers of neutrons. That core is called a neutron star.

Which stars will end up as white dwarfs, and which as neutron stars? In the 1930s, the Indian-born American astronomer Subrahmanyan Chandrasekhar answered that question. Any star that ends its life with a mass of less than 1.4 solar masses (the mass of our Sun), he said, will become a white dwarf. Any star with a mass greater than 1.4 solar masses will become a neutron star. There are, however, a few very important exceptions.

Formation of a Black Hole

The stars for which the preceding life-and-death story does not apply are the very heaviest of stars. Astronomers have calculated that a star that ends its life with more than about 2.5 solar masses cannot survive even as a neutron star. Gravitational forces will be so strong that all matter within the star's dead core will be crushed into a point. Millions and millions of tons of matter will be forced together into an unimaginably small point. Indeed, astronomers say that the final volume of the star that remains is no larger than a single point, a point to which they have given the name singularity. That point, containing enormous amounts of mass in what amounts to zero volume, is a black hole.

What a remarkable conclusion! What this means is that very large stars end their lives by producing two of the most amazing events in the universe. One is the brilliant explosion of a supernova. The other is the unmeasurable force of a black hole.

This artist's impression shows a black hole and a blue giant star in a binary star system. To date, scientists can only imagine what black holes actually look like.

CHAPTER 5

"A BLACK HOLE HAS NO HAIR"

Black holes can be described fairly easily using equations and diagrams. But those equations and diagrams probably do not answer one basic question in your mind: What does a black hole actually look like?

One way to answer that question is to consider the simplest possible model of a black hole that scientists can imagine. This model may not match black holes in the real world exactly, but it is a good place to begin understanding what black holes are like. The illustration on page 48 shows the simplest model of a black hole.

The ring labeled "event horizon" in that diagram represents an imaginary boundary for the black hole. Anything that falls within the event horizon will be captured forever—pulled into the black hole by its gravitational attraction. That gravitational attraction is so strong that nothing can escape from it. An object is simply attracted more and more strongly as it travels closer and closer to the very center of the black hole itself.

Imagine that a spacecraft is traveling in the vicinity of the black hole shown below. As long as the spacecraft stays outside the event horizon, it has an opportunity to escape from the black hole. It can increase its speed enough to overcome the

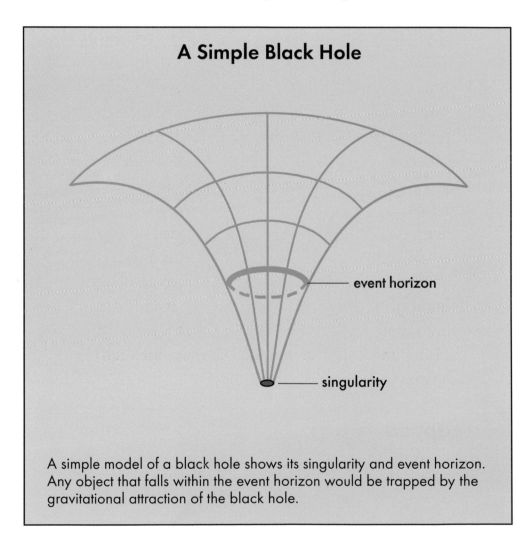

A Simple Black Hole

event horizon

singularity

A simple model of a black hole shows its singularity and event horizon. Any object that falls within the event horizon would be trapped by the gravitational attraction of the black hole.

gravitational attraction of the black hole. But once it passes over the event horizon, it has passed the point of no return. No amount of increase in its speed can carry it back across the event horizon and away from the black hole.

So what does one find *inside* the event horizon? Imagine that a wayward spacecraft has crossed the event horizon. As it travels toward the center of the black hole, gravitational forces become stronger and stronger. The sections of the spacecraft are crushed together as if they had been placed in some giant trash compactor. The closer the squashed spacecraft gets to the center of the black hole, the more tightly it is compacted.

At the very center of the black hole, gravitational attraction becomes so great that the spacecraft is reduced from its original size to the size of a car and then to the size of a loaf of bread and then to the size of a pinhead. Eventually it is squeezed into an object with virtually no volume at all.

This concept is perhaps the most difficult idea of all about black holes. A spacecraft weighing several tons and taking up the space of a large airplane has been reduced to an object that occupies almost no space whatsoever, although it still has a mass of many tons. But that, after all, is what black holes are all about: packing unbelievable amounts of mass into zero or almost-zero volumes.

The Disappearance of Properties

So what would something look like that had passed through the event horizon of a black hole? The answer to that question was discovered in the 1960s by the Russian scientist

Vitaly Ginzburg. Ginzburg theorized that anything that passed through the event horizon would lose all physical properties by which we recognize objects, except three. The object, he said, would no longer have shape, volume, color, or temperature. The only properties that would be retained by the object are mass, electrical charge, and rotation (the ability to spin).

Suppose that a spacecraft passing a black hole threw out some garbage, consisting of apple cores, computer diskettes, and empty ball point pens. As those objects passed through the event horizon, they would be destroyed. All that would remain would be the atoms of which the materials were comprised. Anyone inside the black hole (which is impossible) would simply see atomic fragments of the apple cores, diskettes, and pens—all of which would look completely alike. This is why scientists say that objects within a black hole "have no memory."

Imaginative scientists have described this condition by saying that "black holes have no hair." That expression means that nothing sticks out of a black hole (like the hair on a person's head) that tells us anything about what's actually inside the hole.

Some astronomers theorize about different kinds of black holes. For example, one kind of black hole might have mass (as all black holes do), but no electrical charge and no rotation. A second kind of black hole might have mass and electrical charge, but no rotation. Both these examples, however, are purely theoretical. Most astronomers have good reason to believe that neither kind of black hole could ever exist in the real world.

Patriot and Genius: Karl Schwarzschild

In November 1915, scientist Albert Einstein announced his general theory of relativity. Einstein's theory was one of the most important breakthroughs in the history of science. His bold new approach to physics encouraged other scientists to explore questions about the natural world in entirely new ways.

One of these physicists was a German by the name of Karl Schwarzschild. Schwarzschild was born in Frankfurt-am-Main on October 9, 1873. He studied physics at the universities of Strasbourg and Munich and earned his Ph.D. in 1896. Five years later, he became director of the University of Göttingen.

When World War I began, Schwarzschild volunteered for military service. In his spare time, when he was not solving problems related to artillery, he worked on some new problems suggested by Einstein's theory. One of those problems was the bending of light caused by strong gravitational forces. Einstein's theory had suggested that light will be bent when it passes through a region of strong gravitational attraction. What would happen, Schwarzschild asked, if a light beam were to pass close to a point in space where the gravitational force were not only great, but were enormously large?

Schwarzschild's calculations produced some remarkable results. He found that space would curve in upon itself at such a point and a light beam traveling across the space would disappear into the central point. He also found that this effect could occur not only at a single point of intense gravitational force, but also across a broader range of space. The only condition was that the ratio between the mass of an object and its volume had to be large enough to create a very strong gravitational force. For example, if Earth could be shrunk to a diameter of one centimeter (retaining its mass), it would bend light in upon itself also. In modern terms, one would say that the Earth had become a black hole.

Schwarzschild's discovery was important because it was the first theoretical proof that an object such as a black hole could really exist. The imaginary concepts of Michell and Laplace had, at last, been given a sound scientific basis. In honor of his discovery, the simplest forms of black holes are today called Schwarzschild black holes.

Black Holes in the Real World

Scientists know that the simplest possible model of black holes, as seen on page 48, is almost certainly not correct. For one thing, all stars rotate on their own axes, the way the Earth rotates on its axis. So the black hole formed from a dead star must rotate also. You could compare a rotating black hole to water draining out of a bathtub, swirling around in a whirlpool as it enters the drain. Similarly, a rotating black hole swirls around, sweeping up objects within its event horizon and dragging them into its center.

Swirling water funnels, like black holes, can pull passing objects into their centers.

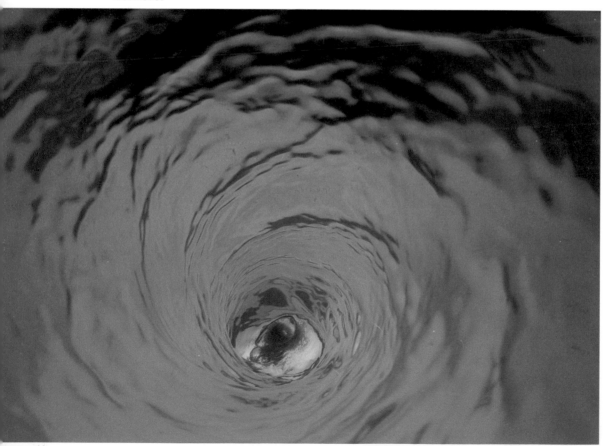

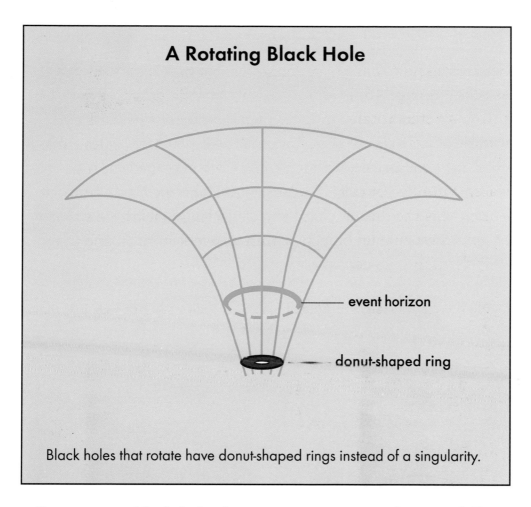

A Rotating Black Hole

event horizon

donut-shaped ring

Black holes that rotate have donut-shaped rings instead of a singularity.

But rotating black holes have some properties that are different from stationary black holes. For one thing, the center of a rotating black hole does not consist of a singularity, but of a donut-shaped ring, as shown in the illustration above. Objects that pass across the event horizon are sucked into the ring, where they disappear forever.

But some scientists have raised an interesting possibility. It might be, they suggest, that objects can pass through the middle of the ring. Then they could enter the wormhole, pass out

Magical Numbers

The scientist whose name is perhaps most closely associated with black hole research today is Stephen Hawking, professor of mathematics at Cambridge University. For three decades, Hawking has pondered the meaning of mathematical equations that describe black holes.

His most important contribution has probably been the notion of mini-black holes. Scientific research on mini-black holes promises to bring together what we know about the largest, most dramatic event in the history of the universe—the Big Bang—and the tiny particles that

Stephen Hawking is considered to be one of the greatest scientists of this century.

make up protons and neutrons called quarks.

Hawking was born in Oxford, England, on January 8, 1942. He attended Oxford University, where he received a degree in physics, and Cambridge University, where he received his Ph.D. While just in his twenties, Hawking began to show some of the brilliance for which he is now well known. For example, as a student at Oxford, Hawking impressed his classmates by spending only three hours working out thirteen difficult physics problems, while they needed the entire week that was assigned by the professor to do them.

At about the same time Hawking was being noticed by his peers, however, he began to develop a medical disorder known as amyotrophic lateral sclerosis (ALS), also known as Lou Gehrig's disease. The illness damages nerves that control voluntary motion, reducing a person's ability to speak or move. At first, doctors told Hawking that he could only expect to live a few years. Now, over 30 years later, Hawking continues to live with ALS.

Today, Hawking gets around in a wheelchair. He is able to think as well as he ever has. But he has to rely on an electronic device to convert his thoughts and mathematical equations into words. To express an idea, he selects words from a computer menu or he taps out letters on an electronic keyboard, one at a time. The computer then converts the letters and words into artificial sounds. The method is slow, but there is a certain majesty in hearing some of the most profound thoughts in the world expressed by Hawking's voice synthesizer. (Hawking once said that his synthesizer—created by a U.S. computer engineer—has an American accent.) Despite the artificial voice, Hawking's humor and grace are still clearly evident.

In addition to his theoretical work, Hawking has written a number of popular books for the non-scientist. One of those, *A Brief History of Time*, was a best seller. Despite a condition that many people might regard as a handicap, Hawking continues to astonish both his colleagues and the general public with his imaginative and groundbreaking ideas about the universe.

of the white hole on the opposite side of the wormhole, and emerge into an alternative universe. These scientists argue that black holes might be used for time travel after all!

This argument forms the basis of many science-fiction stories. In such stories, clever space travelers pass through the event

A still from the 1979 movie *The Black Hole* depicts a spaceship—the *U.S.S. Cygnus*—about to enter a swirling black hole.

horizon and aim their spaceships toward the center of the black hole's inner ring. They somehow avoid being swallowed up by the ring itself and travel on to another time and place.

Such tales make wonderful stories. But most scientists do not believe that such trips are possible. They argue that anything passing over the event horizon would be exposed to such strong gravitational forces that they would be destroyed and only the atoms of which they are made would remain. Even before entering the black hole itself, all that would remain of a human visitor and his or her spacecraft would be the individual protons and neutrons of which they are made. Space travelers and their ships might get through the black hole, most scientists argue, but they would do so in the unrecognizable form of protons and neutrons.

Black holes are one of the most exciting objects of study in modern astronomy. Many scientists believe that the information we learn from black holes will revolutionize much of what we know about our universe. Perhaps the most fascinating point about black holes today is the differences of opinion that remain about them. Do they truly provide a possible means of travel through space and time? Could they someday be a virtually endless supply of energy for our civilization? Enough disagreement remains among scientists for all of these possibilities to remain the focus of much scholarly discussion. Fortunately, they also provide science-fiction writers with the raw material for ever newer and more intriguing guesses about the world of tomorrow. And who knows? Science fiction has long made predictions about worlds of the future that few people thought possible. Perhaps black holes also will someday be of value to humans in ways that no one today can possibly imagine.

alternative universe A region of space believed by some astronomers to exist. Similar to our own universe, but not presently capable of being studied by methods available.

astronomy The study of the universe, its origins, and the materials of which it is made.

atomic fission A nuclear reaction in which a large particle breaks down into two or more smaller particles.

Big Bang A theory that explains the origin and evolution of the universe, starting with a cataclysmic explosion.

binary star A pair of stars that stay together and orbit around each other because of the gravitational force between them.

black hole A region of the universe in which a very large mass is concentrated into a very small (essentially zero) volume. Scientists still disagree as to whether black holes actually exist.

blue supergiant A very large, hot, bright star, which is near the end of its time of burning hydrogen in its core.

electron A tiny negatively charged particle found in atoms.

escape velocity The speed that an object must reach before it can escape the gravitational attraction of Earth, the Moon, or some other body in space.

event horizon The boundary surrounding a black hole beyond which nothing—neither mass nor energy—can escape.

galaxy A large group of stars, dust, and gas held together by gravitational attraction.

general theory of relativity A theory developed by Albert Einstein in 1915 that attempts to explain the attraction of objects for each other in the universe.

gravitational attraction *See gravity.*

gravitational lens A visual effect produced in the skies when a body with a very large mass bends light rays that pass near it.

gravity The force of attraction that exists between two bodies.

infrared radiation A form of radiation, similar to visible light, but with longer wavelengths.

Large Magellanic Cloud A galaxy relatively close to, but smaller than, the Milky Way galaxy.

mass The amount of material contained within an object.

Milky Way The common name for the galaxy in which our Sun and solar system is located.

mini-black holes Very small black holes, about the size of an atom. Mini-black holes are also called primordial black holes.

neutrino A very small subatomic particle that has no charge and either no mass or very small mass.

neutron A small uncharged particle found in all atoms except hydrogen.

neutron star A very dense object left after a large star has exploded and given off most of its mass.

nuclear fusion A nuclear reaction in which two or more small particles combine to make one larger particle.

parallel universe *See alternative universe.*

planetary nebula A cloud of gas and dust thrown off and then heated to glowing by a star in the last stages of its life.

proton A small positively charged particle found in all atoms.

quantum physics A field of science developed in the 1920s to describe the behavior of very small particles.

quark A tiny particle that makes up protons and neutrons.

radio waves A form of radiation, similar to visible light, but with longer wavelengths.

red supergiant A very large and bright red star. This is one of the last stages a star goes through before it becomes a supernova.

rotation The act of spinning around a central axis.

singularity A point in space that has very large mass and no volume.

supernova An enormous explosion that occurs in space during which a star expels all or most of its mass.

wavelength The distance between any two peaks or valleys in the waves of some form of radiation.

white dwarf A very dense star in the last stages of its life.

white hole A region thought to exist at the opposite end of a wormhole from a black hole.

wormhole A region in space that connects a black hole with a corresponding white hole.

X rays A form of radiation, similar to visible light, but with shorter wavelengths.

FURTHER READING

Asimov, Isaac. *Mysteries of Deep Space: Black Holes, Pulsars, and Quasars,* Revised Edition. Milwaukee: Gareth Stevens, Inc., 1994.

Branley, Franklyn. *Mysteries of the Universe.* New York: Lodestar Books, 1984.

_____. *Superstar: The Supernova of 1987.* New York: HarperCollins Children's Books, 1990.

Clay, Rebecca. *Stars and Galaxies.* New York: Twenty-First Century Books, 1997.

Cole, Ron. *Stephen Hawking: Solving the Mysteries of the Universe.* Chatham, NJ: Raintree Steck-Vaughn, 1996.

Couper, Heather and Nigel Henbest. *Black Holes.* New York: Dorling Kindersley, 1996.

Darling, David. *The Stars: From Birth to Black Holes.* New York: Macmillan, 1987.

George, Michael. *Stars.* Mankato, MN: Creative Education, Inc., 1992.

Haslam, Andrew. *Universe.* New York: Thomson Learning, 1995.

Henderson, Harry. *The Importance of Stephen Hawking.* San Diego, CA: Lucent Books, 1995.

Stannard, Russell. *Our Universe: A Guide to What's Out There.* New York: Larousse Kingfisher Chambers, Inc., 1995.

Stars (*Voyage Through the Universe* series). Richmond, VA: Time-Life Books, Inc., 1992.

To see a list of frequently asked questions and answers about black holes visit the Black Holes FAQ page at http://physics7. berkeley.edu/BHfaq.html

To see brief animated movies on black holes visit Our Scientific Movies page. It is sponsored by the NCSA Relativity Group and can be found at http://jean-luc.ncsa.uiuc.edu/Movies/movies.html

The Black Holes and Neutron Stars page gives non-technical explanations about black holes and neutron stars. It can be found on the web at http://www.safe.net/cmmiller/blkhle.html

The High Energy Astrophysics Science Archive Research Center (HEASARC) sponsors a supernova web site that explains what a supernova is and shows an artist's concept of one occuring. Visit it at http://legacy.gsfc.nasa.gov/docs/blackhole.html

The web page Black Holes and Mysteries of the Cosmos has "everything you wanted to know about Black Holes and Mysteries of the Cosmos, but were afraid to ask!" It also has links to other sites about black holes. The address is http://www.geocities.com/CapeCanaveral/3001/

SOURCES

"Biggest Black Hole." *Science*, February 16, 1996.

"Black Hole." *McGraw-Hill Encyclopedia of Science & Technology*, 7th edition. New York: McGraw-Hill Book Company, 1992, Volume 2.

"Black Holes Galore." *Astronomy*, February 1996.

Chown, Marcus. "Why Small Black Holes Are Just Hippies." *New Scientist*, February 24, 1996.

Cowen, Ron. "Hubble Finds Off-center Black Hole." *Science News*, December 15, 1995.

Driedger, Walter C. "The Care and Feeding of Black Holes." *Astronomy*, May 1995.

"From Black Holes to Quarks." *Astronomy*, October 1995.

Hawking, Stephen. *Black Holes and Baby Universes and Other Essays*. New York: Bantam Books, 1993.

Kaufmann, William J., III. *Black Holes and Warped Timespace*. San Francisco: W. H. Freeman, 1979.

Luminet, Jean-Pierre. *Black Holes*. Cambridge: Cambridge University Press, 1992.

"A Quiet Beast." *Astronomy*, September 1995.

"Seeing Close to a Black Hole." *Astronomy*, July 1995.

Thorne, Kip S. *Black Holes and Time Warps: Einstein's Outrageous Legacy*. New York: W. W. Norton, 1994.

"Time Travel." *National Geographic World*, March 1995.

Von Baeyer, Hans Christian. "Black Holes, Ants, and Roller Coasters." *Discover*, July 1995.

INDEX